Author:
Alex Woolf studied history at Essex University, England. He is the author of over 60 books for children, including *The Science of Acne and Warts: The Itchy Truth About Skin, You Wouldn't Want to Live Without Bees!,* and *You Wouldn't Want to Live Without Vegetables!*

Series creator:
David Salariya was born in Dundee, Scotland. He has illustrated a wide range of books and has created and designed many new series for publishers in the UK and overseas. David established The Salariya Book Company in 1989. He lives in Brighton, England, with his wife, illustrator Shirley Willis, and their son, Jonathan.

Artist:
Bryan Beach

Editor:
Jacqueline Ford

© The Salariya Book Company Ltd MMXVIII
No part of this publication may be reproduced in whole or in part, or stored in a retrieval system, or transmitted in any form or by any means, electronic, mechanical, photocopying, recording, or otherwise, without written permission of the publisher. For information regarding permission, write to the copyright holder.

Published in Great Britain in 2018 by
The Salariya Book Company Ltd
25 Marlborough Place, Brighton BN1 1UB

ISBN-13: 978-0-531-25830-9 (lib. bdg.) 978-0-531-26900-8 (pbk.)

All rights reserved.
Published in 2018 in the United States
by Franklin Watts
An imprint of Scholastic Inc.

A CIP catalog record for this book is available
from the Library of Congress.

Printed and bound in China.
Printed on paper from sustainable sources.
1 2 3 4 5 6 7 8 9 10 R 27 26 25 24 23 22 21 20 19 18

SCHOLASTIC, FRANKLIN WATTS, and associated logos are trademarks and/or registered trademarks of Scholastic Inc.

PAPER FROM
SUSTAINABLE
FORESTS

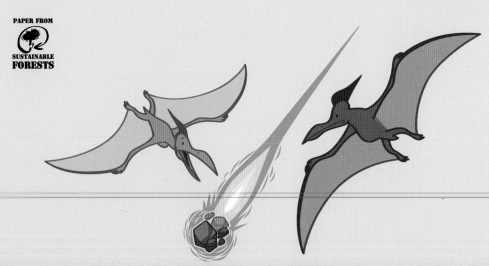

The Science of Flying Reptiles

The Terrifying Truth About the Pterosaurs

written by
Alex Woolf

Illustrated by
Bryan Beach

Franklin Watts®
An Imprint of Scholastic Inc.

Contents

Preondactylus

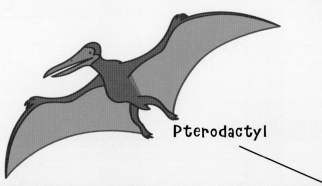

Pterodactyl

| Triassic: 252–201 mya | Jurassic: 201–145 mya |

Mya = Million years ago

Introduction

While the dinosaurs roamed the earth, another species ruled the skies. These were the pterosaurs. They weren't birds, but flying reptiles. In fact, the word *pterosaur* means "winged lizard." They appeared around 228 million years ago, and were the first animals to fly, besides insects.

There were at least 130 kinds of pterosaur, from tiny sparrow-sized creatures to giants as big as a light aircraft. These expert fliers swooped and soared through the sky. They were magnificent hunters, diving for fish, snapping up insects in the air, or dining on baby dinosaurs.

The pterosaurs were not themselves dinosaurs, though they lived at the same time and shared a common ancestor. While dinosaurs have their limbs under their body, pterosaurs, like lizards and crocodiles, have limbs that stick out from the side.

In this book we will discover all about these awesome creatures, how they lived, how they hunted, and why they eventually died out.

Quetzalcoatlus

Cretaceous: 145-65 mya

Throat Pouch

One pterosaur, called the Ikrandraco avatar, had a throat pouch like a modern-day pelican, which it used for storing food. The Ikrandraco flew low over lakes and rivers, catching fish by letting its lower jaw skim through the water.

That might not fit in my throat pouch.

Some pterosaurs had inflatable air sacs in their wings as part of their breathing system.

Key Features

Pterosaurs evolved a number of features that made them first-class fliers and hunters. They had streamlined bodies with long necks; enormous wings; and powerful beaks, often lined with razor-sharp teeth. Like birds, they had hollow, air-filled bones, making them light and well suited to flying. Early pterosaurs had long tails that helped steer them through the air like a rudder. Pterosaurs also spent time on the ground, walking on their hind limbs and forelimbs. To take off, they used their powerful forelimbs to vault into the air. Once aloft, they could reach speeds of up to 75 miles per hour (120 kilometers per hour).

Ptummy empty. Ptime to dig into something ptasty!

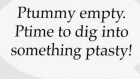

Wings

Pterosaur wings had two parts: a front part attached to the wrist and shoulder, and a much larger rear part that stretched from the extremely long fourth finger of each arm along the sides of the body to the ankles. Some species had a third part stretching between the legs.

Baby pterosaurs (known as flaplings) were born with well-developed wings and could fly soon after hatching from their eggs.

On the Ground

Fossil footprints show that pterosaurs were probably good walkers and runners. They walked in an erect posture with their wings folded and their limbs positioned beneath their bodies.

Yes, we can walk, too!

Famous Fossil Finds

Paleontologists don't know how pterosaurs developed flight. However, the fossil of a small archosaur called Scleromochlus may provide a clue. It was found in Scotland by the naturalist William Taylor in 1907. Scleromochlus was a tree dweller with a skull similar to those of pterosaurs, and it may have been able to glide.

First Discovery

No complete example of an adult Pterodactyl has ever been found.

In the mid-1700s, a very strange-looking fossil was dug up in Germany. At first, paleontologists assumed it was a sea creature, imagining its long arms were used as flippers. Then, a naturalist called Georges Cuvier suggested that the flippers were wings and this creature could fly! He called it Pterodactyl, meaning "winged finger." Cuvier had identified the first pterosaur. He believed Pterodactyl was a reptile. Others argued it was a bat-like mammal. Still others continued to insist it was a sea creature. Cuvier won the argument.

First grow more teeth!

Flapling to Adult

Pterodactyls grew slowly and steadily through their lives, much like crocodiles and turtles, and unlike birds. Younger Pterodactyls had few teeth and fed on insects; adults had around 90 narrow conical teeth, and fed on fish.

It's a reptile.

It's a bat.

It's a sea animal.

Just call me Terry.

8

Stuck in the Mud

Pterodactyls lived in the Jurassic Period, around 150 million years ago. Many of their fossils have been found in Bavaria, Germany. During the Jurassic Period, this area was swampy wetland. Some creatures that fell in the wetland became buried in soft mud. As the mud slowly turned to rock, their bodies became fossils.

Oh no! I may be turning into a fossil!

Anatomy

The Pterodactyl was a relatively small pterosaur, around the size of a modern heron, with an estimated adult wingspan of 3 feet (1 meter). It had a long, curved neck, a long skull, large eyes, a pointed beak with many small teeth, and a very short tail.

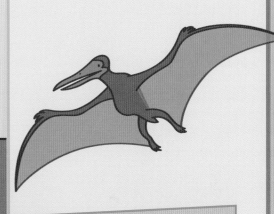

For a long time, all newly discovered flying reptiles were called Pterodactyls— until paleontologists realized that Pterodactyls were just one type of flying reptile within a much larger group—the pterosaurs.

Fascinating Fact

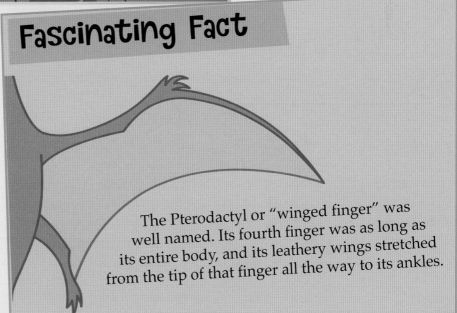

The Pterodactyl or "winged finger" was well named. Its fourth finger was as long as its entire body, and its leathery wings stretched from the tip of that finger all the way to its ankles.

Needle-Toothed Night Flier

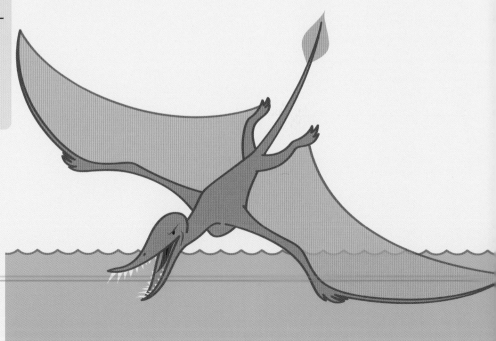

Hunting

Rhamphorhynchus hunted by dragging its hook-shaped beak through the water. When it scooped up a wriggling fish, it would snap its teeth shut, trapping the prey, before tossing it into the food pouch in its throat.

Rhamphorhynchus (meaning "prow beak") was a small but vicious-looking pterosaur from the Jurassic Period. Its jaws were lined with 34 needlelike teeth. The teeth were angled forward and the beak-like tip of its jaws curved upward, suggesting a diet of fish. It had large eyes (helping it see at night), a short neck, and a long, thin tail with a diamond-shaped flap of skin at the end, which it used as a rudder when flying. This was one of the first pterosaurs to be discovered.

An examination of Rhamphorhynchus's eye bones suggest it was a night hunter. If it was cold-blooded—paleontologists aren't sure—it could have warmed up at night by hugging rocks, which retain the sun's heat.

Flying

Rhamphorhynchus was one of the first pterosaurs to learn to fly by flapping its wings—the earliest ones simply glided from tree to tree. It had long, slender, light wings, giving it strength and speed in flight, and a long tail for stability.

Gliding not good enough for you, eh? Show-off!

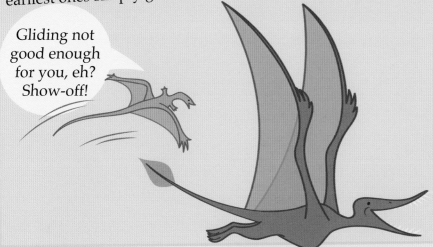

Swimming

When on the ground, Rhamphorhynchus probably swam more than it walked. Its short legs would have made it slow and awkward on land, but its large, broad feet would have been ideal for propelling it through the water.

Think of me as a scary duck.

Rhamphorhynchus flaplings looked a little different from their parents. They had shorter, blunter jaws, and a tail that ended with a sharp-tipped oval.

Famous Fossil Finds

An extraordinary fossil was found in Bavaria, Germany, in 2009. It shows a flying Rhamphorhynchus in the act of scooping up a small fish in its jaws. At that moment, a predatory fish, Aspidorhynchus, lunged out of the water and bit the flying reptile. During the struggle, all three creatures died and sank into the muddy seabed, preserving this action-packed sequence in the rock.

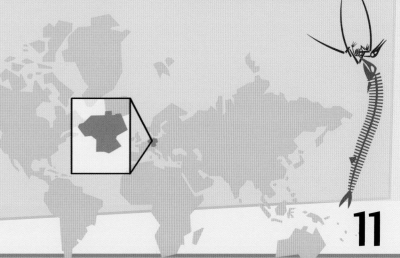

Paleontologists believe Pteranodon flew like a modern albatross, using ocean winds to soar for long periods, with occasional bursts of energetic flapping.

Crested Colossus

The Pteranodon was an astounding pterosaur that lived some 86 million years ago in Kansas, Wyoming, and South Dakota, which was then an inland sea. Unlike earlier pterosaurs like Pterodactyl, Pteranodon was awesomely big, with a wingspan of over 20 feet (6 m). Yet the Pteranodon was almost all head and wings—it had a very small body, only a little bigger than a cat's, and a tiny tail. It had no teeth in its beak, hence its name, which means "toothless wing." Its most distinctive feature was its long, backward-pointing crest at the rear of its skull.

Show-offs

Why did Pteranodon have such a spectacular crest? Paleontologists used to believe it acted as a rudder for the beak. Today, most think it was probably a signaling system males used to attract females—so it was probably brightly colored.

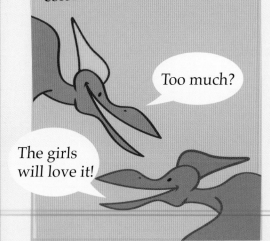

Too much?

The girls will love it!

In the movie *Jurassic Park III*, a Pteranodon carries off a human. Yet paleontologists studying Pteranodon bones have concluded they could not have carried anything heavier than a large fish.

Ducking and Diving

Pteranodon probably hunted while swimming. With its long neck and beak, it could reach a depth of almost 3 feet (1 m) while floating on the surface. It may have plunged even deeper by diving into the water from the air, folding back its wings like a modern gannet.

Where did he go?

Fish Teeth Fiasco

The first Pteranodon remains were discovered in Kansas in 1870 by Othniel Marsh. Nearby, Marsh found some teeth, and because Pterodactyls had teeth, he assumed they belonged to Pteranodon. Only later did he realize they were fish teeth.

This is a fish tooth.

Oh no!

Survival Tactics

Pteranodons avoided attack by carnivorous dinosaurs by nesting on small offshore islands. They had to be careful, though, since the sea was also full of fierce predators, like long-necked plesiosaurs.

How Big?

Quetzalcoatlus was truly gargantuan. It had a wingspan of 36 feet (11 m) when flying, it was 26 feet (8 m) long, its neck measured 10 feet (3 m), and its legs were 7 feet (2.1 m) long. Its beak alone was longer than an adult human!

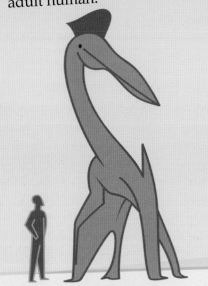

Some paleontologists have argued that Quetzalcoatlus was too heavy to fly and may have been flightless—like modern penguins and ostriches.

Size of an Aircraft

With its 36-foot (11 m) wingspan, Quetzalcoatlus was the size of a light aircraft and the largest creature ever to fly. It lived in North America between 68 million and 65 million years ago—the final era of the dinosaurs—and was one of the last known pterosaurs. Quetzalcoatlus had a very long neck, a sharp, toothless beak, and a long, bony crest on its head. With its light body and enormous wingspan, it could travel vast distances, riding the air currents and breezes with barely a flap of its wings.

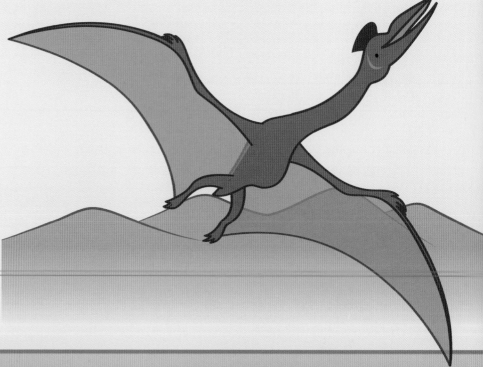

How Did It Fly?

I hope it's high enough!

Due to its colossal size, many paleontologists have pondered how Quetzalcoatlus got off the ground. Did it launch itself with its powerful front legs, or did it jump off a high cliff? Experts have calculated that once airborne, the pterosaur could fly at up to 80 miles per hour (130 kph) for 7 to 10 days at a time, at altitudes of up to 14,700 feet (4,500 m).

What Did It Eat?

It'll take a lot of these to fill me up!

Paleontologists disagree about Quetzalcoatlus's diet. Some argue it lived like a vulture, feeding on dinosaur corpses. Others say its slender jaws would have been better adapted to probing sand and mud for fish, crabs, and worms, rather like oversized storks.

Despite its huge size, Quetzalcoatlus was lightly built, with hollow bones, and probably weighed no more than 220 pounds (100 kilograms). Some paleontologists, who believe it was flightless, say it could have weighed up to 1,190 pounds (540 kg).

Famous Fossil Finds

Geology student Douglas Lawson discovered the first evidence of Quetzalcoatlus in 1971 at Big Bend National Park in Texas. He found the fossilized remains of part of a wing, and estimated a creature with a wingspan of over 33 feet (10 m).

Thalassodromeus had a crest three times larger than the rest of its skull when seen from the side. In fact, it had one of the largest crests of any known vertebrate.

Curious Crests

Many pterosaurs evolved head crests of various shapes and sizes. Paleontologists have speculated that these may have been used for aerodynamics, to regulate body temperature, or, like a rooster's comb, to attract members of the opposite sex. Some crests may even have been used as a threat or a weapon. The longest of all pterosaur crests belonged to Nyctosaurus. This bony, L-shaped adornment could be up to 1.6 feet (0.5 m) in length, four times longer than its owner's skull. Similar to the way stags use their antlers during mating season, Nyctosaurus males may have used their crests as weapons against other males in midair battles.

Skin Sail?

Some paleontologists suggest the Nyctosaurus crest was like the mast of a sail made of skin, helping the pterosaur propel or steer itself through the sky. By turning its head, it could catch a breeze like a sailboat.

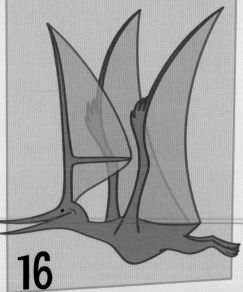

Go ahead! Attack me! I dare you!

Tapejara

Another pterosaur displaying a spectacular crest was Tapejara from South America. Its huge head ornament could grow up to almost 3 feet (1 m) in length. It was formed from two bones with a flap of skin stretched across, and was probably brightly colored to attract mates.

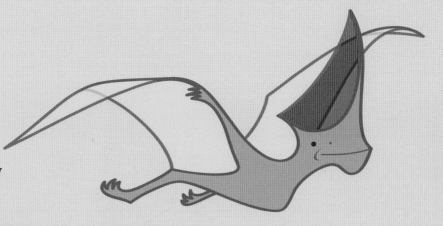

Keeping Cool

Thalassodromeus had an elaborate crest filled with blood vessels. This suggests the crest was used for cooling purposes, much as an African elephant uses its ears. It's also possible it changed color seasonally, allowing its owner to signal to the opposite sex.

The Seripterus was unusual in having three crests. It had one on top of its skull and two more lower down on its snout. It is the only one in its family (rhamphorhynchoid pterosaurs) to have a skull crest.

I think I'll go pink this season....

Can You Believe It?

The pterosaur Tupandactylus is famous for its enormous sail-like crest. In 2008, a research team built an aerial drone (pterodrone) to mimic the pterosaur, trying to show how it might have used its sail for maneuvering and also as a sensing device.

Deep-Beaked Demon

The deep jaws of Dimorphodon were packed with pointy teeth for spearing fish, and its spacious mouth contained plenty of room for a big catch. The pterosaur had 40 small, sharp teeth along the sides of its jaws, and two larger piercing teeth at the front—hence its name, which means "two-form tooth."

I'm the best!

Big mouth!

Dimorphodon's big beak may have been patterned, like a puffin's or a toucan's, to impress females during the breeding season.

Bizarre Beaks

Many pterosaurs had unusually shaped beaks. Pterodaustro, for example, had a long, upward-curving beak. This South American pterosaur resembled in some ways the modern flamingo. Like the flamingo, it was probably a filter feeder. It would dip its curved beak into the water, and any plankton or other tiny aquatic creatures would get stuck in the bristle-like teeth lining its lower jaw. Blunt teeth in its upper jaw would then brush the food out of the bristles and down its throat. Since the food it ate, such as shrimp, was pinkish in color, pterodaustro might well have been pink—just like flamingos!

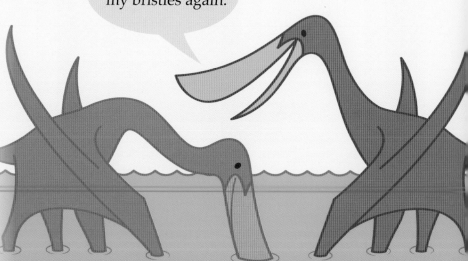

I got food stuck in my bristles again.

Flying Crocodile

Cearadactylus had jaws similar to a crocodile's. At the tip of its jaws was a semicircle of interlocking needlelike teeth, which it used to trap fish. The other teeth were smaller and blunter, which suggests Cearadactylus didn't chew, but swallowed its prey whole.

Chewing is for wimps!

Fish-Spearing Fiend

The beak of Dsungaripterus, a pterosaur of the Early Cretaceous, curved upward at the tip. This probably helped it to spear fish, or pry off shellfish clinging to the undersides of rocks.

No fish or mollusk is safe from my beak.

Dsungaripterus's beak contained bony, knob-like teeth. When it shut its jaws tight, these teeth would exert crushing power, cracking open shellfish like a nutcracker.

Fascinating Fact

Ornithocheirus, the largest pterosaur of the Middle Cretaceous Period, had semicircular crests on its beak. These got thinner toward the tip, making it streamlined like the prow of a boat as it pushed its beak through the water hunting for fish.

19

Furry Fliers

The bodies of some pterosaurs, like Jeholopterus and *Sordes pilosus*, were covered in fur. This makes them sound almost cute, but these creatures were deadly predators, and probably about as cute as a vampire bat! So what was this fur? It was made up of masses of hairlike filaments called pycnofibers. These may have been primitive feathers, although they did not appear on the wings, only the heads and bodies, so they probably didn't help pterosaurs fly. Some paleontologists believe pycnofibers helped keep pterosaurs warm.

The fur that covered these pterosaurs was most likely for insulation, so this might mean they were warm-blooded, like birds.

Agile Hunter

Jeholopterus was an owl-sized pterosaur living in northeastern China in the Middle to Late Jurassic Period. It had a big catlike head and long, sharp, curved claws. With its broad, short wings it could bob and weave through branches, snapping at insects with its small jaws and tiny, sharp teeth.

He may be furry, but he is NOT cute!

Bloodsucker?

Jeholopterus had long fangs in its top jaw, much larger than the rest of its teeth, and this led some paleontologists to wonder if it was a bloodsucker. Perhaps it used its powerful claws to latch onto dinosaurs and feed on their blood. Most experts are doubtful about this theory, since there is no actual evidence for it.

I think something's sucking my blood.

Well, it can't be Jeholopterus!

Sordes pilosus means "hairy filth," a reference to evil spirits in local folklore. This was an early pterosaur, first appearing in the Late Jurassic Period. It had a short jaw and a long tail—two features that changed in pterosaurs as they evolved.

A possible purpose of the fur was to reduce the sound of the pterosaur in flight, making it easier for the pterosaur to surprise its prey.

Famous Fossil Finds

The first *Sordes pilosus* fossil was unearthed in 1971 by Aleksandr Sharov in the foothills of the Karatau Mountains in Kazakhstan. It was the first pterosaur found to have a fur-like covering. Much later, in 2009, the hair filaments were named pycnofibers.

Fish Food

Although pterosaurs often fed upon fish, sometimes it worked the other way around. The remains of tiny pterosaur Preondactylus have been found in some fish poop.

I'm going to eat you!

No, I'm going to eat you!

Tiny Terrors

By the Late Cretaceous Period, pterosaurs had evolved into enormous beasts like Pteranodon and Quetzalcoatlus. But in their earlier history, pterosaurs were a lot smaller, and some were even as small as sparrows. These puny predators mainly lived in forests and caught insects in their tiny, toothless jaws. Being small meant they may have been preyed on themselves. There is evidence from their eye bones that many were active at night—possibly because it made them safer from predators. As dinosaurs evolved into the first birds, they may have out-competed the smaller pterosaurs, many of which became extinct.

Preondactylus was one of the earliest pterosaurs, and this may explain its very short wings in relation to its body length.

Just you wait till I evolve!

Teeny-Tiny Tree Climber

Nemicolopterus is currently one of the world's tiniest known pterosaurs, with a wingspan of just 10 inches (25 centimeters). Its curved claws suggest it perched on branches and possibly even climbed trees.

You're not much bigger than I am!

Fossil Fraud

Dendrorhynchoides confused paleontologists when they first saw its fossils. Clearly this tiny creature belonged to the short-tailed anurognathid family of pterosaurs, yet it had a long tail. The reason? Cunning fossil dealers had added a fake tail to make it look better and increase its value.

It'll look better with a tail—and maybe a nice pair of ears....

Dendrorhynchoides, an insect-eating pterosaur, had the flattest, widest skull of all pterosaurs, and eyes that popped up above its head like a frog's.

Survival Tactics

Mini-pterosaurs like Nemicolopterus spent their entire lives in the forest canopy, far above the ground. Here they could dine on insects while avoiding big, aggressive, ground-based predators.

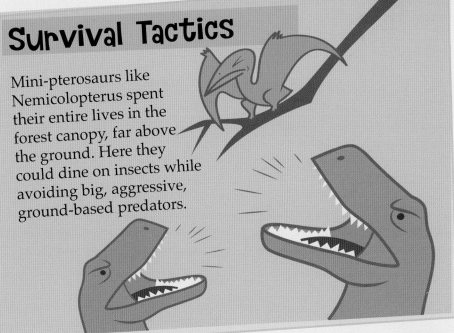

Weird and Wonderful

As we've seen, pterosaurs came in all sizes and forms—huge and small, toothy and toothless, tailed and tailless. Some had huge crests, others had odd-shaped beaks. Some flaunted other weird and wonderful features. Azhdarcho, for example, had a long, massive head and beak, perched on the end of a long, thin neck and short body. Its odd look has led to arguments between paleontologists about how it fed: Did it skim for fish, or poke around for food on the ground? Those arguments still go on.

In 2014, paleontologists in southern Brazil unearthed a whole flock of pterosaurs with bizarre, butterfly-like head crests. They named the new species Caiuajara.

Missing Link

Darwinopterus, discovered in 2009, had the body, wings, and long tail of early rhamphorhynchoid pterosaurs, and the head and neck of the later pterodactyloids. It was the missing link between the two kinds of pterosaurs, showing how they evolved.

I feel a little mixed up!

Forget it! You'll never figure out how I eat!

Hatzegopteryx was found in Hatzeg Basin, an island during the Cretaceous. Island species tend to be small, so why was this giant there? Maybe it was just passing through when it died.

Toy Finger

For years, paleontologists got so annoyed when they looked at toy pterosaurs. They all looked like Pteranodons with teeth—yet no such creature ever existed! Until, one day, they discovered that one did! They named it Ludodactylus ("toy finger") in honor of all the toymakers they had insulted.

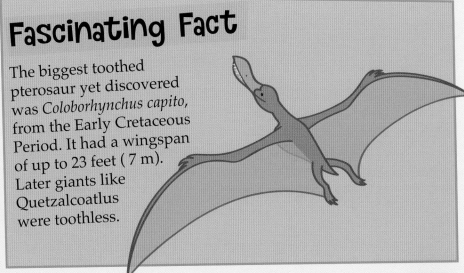

The toymakers were right!

Biggest Ever?

Quetzalcoatlus might have a rival for biggest flying creature ever, and that's Hatzegopteryx. Discovered in 2002, very little fossil material exists, but paleontologists estimate that if this really is a new species, it had a wingspan of 33 to 36 feet (10 to 11 m)!

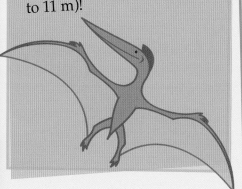

Fascinating Fact

The biggest toothed pterosaur yet discovered was *Coloborhynchus capito*, from the Early Cretaceous Period. It had a wingspan of up to 23 feet (7 m). Later giants like Quetzalcoatlus were toothless.

25

The first birds may have flown with four wings. Birdlike dinosaurs such as Microraptor had long, sturdy feathers on their hind legs, some of which looked like flight feathers. We don't know if these rear wings were used for gliding assistance, steering, or both.

Early Birds

Birds evolved from carnivorous dinosaurs called theropods during the Jurassic Period. Now the pterosaurs had to compete with another creature for domination of the skies. The earliest known birdlike animal is Archaeopteryx. This raven-sized predator retained a lot of dinosaur features, like sharp, pointed teeth; big, clawed feet; and a long, bony tail. Although its arms had developed into feather-covered wings, it still had finger claws. Archaeopteryx was heavy compared to modern birds, and would not have been a good flier. It might have made long leaps, or glided from high places.

First Beak

Confuciusornis was one of the earliest known birds to have a beak and no teeth. It also had the longest feathers compared to its body size of all the primitive birdlike creatures. Yet it probably wasn't a great flier, since it lacked a fan-shaped tail.

Huh! Teeth are so Late Jurassic!

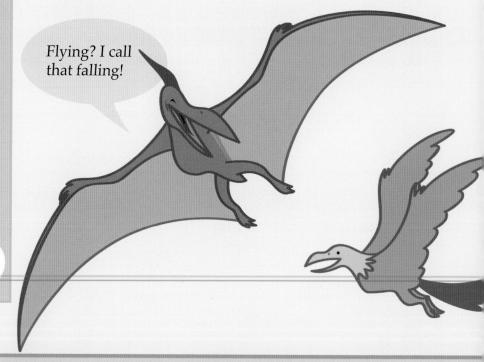

Flying? I call that falling!

Bat-Winged Dinosaur

Yi qi ("strange wing") was a pigeon-sized, feathered dinosaur. It had a long bony rod extending from each wrist, which seemed to have supported a wing of leathery skin, much like on a bat. If true, this makes it the only known dinosaur to have learned to fly without feathered wings.

Am I a bird?
Am I a bat?
No, I'm me!

Scary Penguin

Hesperornis was a big, flightless, prehistoric seabird that looked something like a cross between a penguin and a grebe. It had sharp teeth ideal for catching fish, tiny wings, and was an excellent swimmer.

How did dinosaurs evolve into birds in just 10 million years? A clue to this mystery was unearthed in China in the 1990s: fossils of feather-covered dinosaurs. So dinosaurs evolved feathers long before the first birds came along.

Famous Fossil Finds

When Othniel Marsh discovered the fossil of the prehistoric seabird Ichthyornis in Kansas in 1871, he thought perhaps the fossils of two creatures had gotten mixed up. How else could he explain a bird with teeth? Once he realized it was one creature, his discovery shocked paleontologists. For it proved that birds had evolved from an earlier type of animal, later discovered to be theropods.

27

Extinction

Why did the pterosaurs die out while mammals and birds survived? Many pterosaur species had become very big by the Late Cretaceous, like the dinosaurs. And bigger creatures found it harder to survive the devastation.

Asteroid Crater

Where did the giant asteroid land? The most likely site is the Chicxulub Crater in Mexico, created 65 million years ago. The crater is more than 112 miles (180 km) wide, and scientists estimate it struck with a force of over 100 million megatons!

Around 65 million years ago, something catastrophic happened to Earth. We know this because all the pterosaurs and dinosaurs disappeared relatively suddenly from the fossil record. They became extinct. So what happened? There is strong evidence to suggest that a giant asteroid struck Earth at this time, which would have caused widespread devastation to animal and plant life. Also, around the same period, there was a lot of volcanic activity, causing changes in Earth's atmosphere. So pterosaur extinction may have been caused by an asteroid, volcanoes, or a combination of the two.

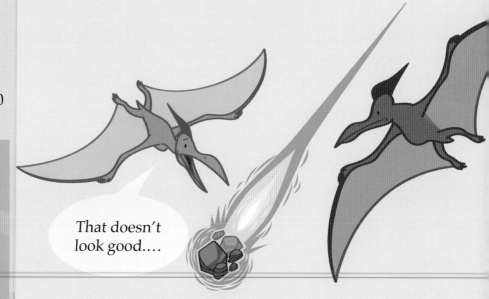

That doesn't look good....

I told you it didn't look good.

Impact Winter

The asteroid impact would have sent up huge amounts of dust into Earth's atmosphere, blocking out the sunlight for months or even years. Temperatures would have fallen, causing many plants and animals to die.

Volcanic Violence

Starting around 66 million years ago, there was an increase in volcanic activity in northern India. The eruptions released dust and poisonous gases into the atmosphere, which may have started killing off the pterosaurs long before the asteroid struck.

What could be worse than this?

A giant rock hitting the planet?

Why didn't small pterosaurs survive? Perhaps because they weren't able to live underground like burrowing mammals, or in water like crocodiles, so they couldn't avoid the worst of the impact.

Fascinating Fact

The mass extinction event 65 million years ago wiped out 75 percent of all life on Earth. But it provided opportunities for other animals. New kinds of mammals emerged, including primates and, eventually, humans. So, without it, we probably wouldn't be here today studying pterosaur fossils!

Glossary

Adornment Something that decorates or makes something else look more attractive.

Aerodynamics The way an object or creature moves through the air.

Air sac A compartment within the lung or some other part of the body containing air.

Aquatic Relating to water.

Archosaur A reptile belonging to a large group that includes dinosaurs and pterosaurs.

Asteroid A rocky body smaller than a planet, which orbits the sun.

Carnivorous Meat-eating.

Cold-blooded Describing animals, such as reptiles and fish, whose body temperature varies depending on the environment.

Cretaceous A period in Earth's history lasting from approximately 145 million to 65 million years ago.

Drone A remote-controlled pilotless aircraft.

Evolve Develop gradually over many generations.

Filament A fine, threadlike object or fiber, especially one found in plants or animals.

Filter feeder An aquatic animal that feeds by filtering out tiny animals or nutrients suspended in water.

Forest canopy The uppermost branches of trees in a forest, forming a more or less continuous layer of foliage.

Fossil The remains of a prehistoric organism embedded in rock and preserved in a petrified (stony) form.

Fossilized Preserved as a fossil.

Fossil record The record of the appearance and evolution of living organisms as understood by the study of fossils.

Insulation A layer of material that protects something from loss of heat.

Invertebrate An animal without a backbone.

Jurassic A period in Earth's history lasting from approximately 201 million to 145 million years ago.

Mammal A warm-blooded, vertebrate animal possessing hair or fur. Female mammals produce milk for their young and usually give birth to live young.

Megaton A unit of explosive power. One megaton is equivalent to one million tons of TNT.

Mollusk A group of invertebrate organisms (lacking a backbone), including snails, slugs, mussels, and octopuses.

Naturalist An expert in natural history.

Ornament A thing whose purpose is to make something look more attractive.

Paleontologist An expert in fossil animals and plants.

Predator An animal that hunts and kills other animals.

Primate A type of mammal, including monkeys, apes, and humans, that have hands, handlike feet, and forward-facing eyes.

Regulate Control or maintain something.

Reptile A cold-blooded vertebrate animal possessing dry, scaly skin, which typically lays eggs on land. Reptiles include snakes, lizards, and crocodiles.

Vertebrate An animal that possesses a backbone.

Warm-blooded Describing animals, such as mammals and birds, who maintain a constant body temperature, typically warmer than their surroundings.

Index